Life's Meanderings

Sudarsana Sarkar

BlueRose Publishers

First Published in June 2020

ISBN: 978-93-90034-78-9

BLUEROSE PUBLISHERS

www.bluerosepublishers.com

info@bluerosepublishers.com

+91 8882 898 898

Cover Design:

Mohd Arif

Typographic Design:

Tanya Raj Upadhyay

Distributed by: BlueRose, Amazon, Flipkart, Shopclues

I DEDICATE THIS BOOK TO ALL THOSE WHO HAVE TRAVELLED WITH ME IN THIS JOURNEY OF LIFE.

Acknowledgement

It is a very heartening moment for me when time has arrived to acknowledge the beautiful contributions of my family and friends to my life's experiences, which have inspired me in many ways, to write. Frankly speaking, without their continuous motivation, I wouldn't have been writing today. I shall remain ever so grateful to you all.

I shall also remain ever thankful to another very special person in my life and it is none other than you, my dear reader! Without you, my creation remains incomplete. What can I say, I can only wish you a very pleasurable read!

Preface

I have been audacious enough to grapple with all the mysteries of life's existence, in the poems, which I have penned. Personally, for me, writing poems is an experience difficult to narrate. It is intoxicating, it is joyful, it is a process of exorcism, at the end of which, there is relief and a strange sense of satisfaction of having lived a life. Life, when seems a burden, then writing a poem is equivalent to ushering peace and balance in the inner world of turbulence.

These poems have dealt with the questions that mankind has been asking himself since the beginning of civilization but the answers his explorative and philosophical mind has thrown back has always been illusive and nothing very concrete. Are we so comfortable in leading ordinary lives, that extremities baffle us and make us behave illogically? Is humanitarianism compromised because we are not tutored to spend sufficient time on reflections? There is a continuous pain which tarries in our minds and we try to forget it through various means of intoxication, wondering all the while about our physical and spiritual selves and their meanings. This has been a mystery relentlessly intriguing the minds of the humankind. For who wants meaninglessness - who can live with it? No one. So man's desperate struggle to find meanings in all his actions and thoughts. So, is he destined to suffer pain, uncertainty and fear, in order to discover the meaning of existence? Nevertheless, does the option still remain to live a meaningless life with a carefree attitude, like the warrior who has promised his physical self to death and his spirits to the air of absolute uncertainty, with absolute certainty hidden in it, in the belief that everything is so temporary that it is useless to suffer pain over anything?

But questions about life never deterred me from tasting life in all its facets. In spite of life being a trouble, who can deny its enchantment, mystery and intoxication? The pain, the trouble, which almost kills our entire being, also makes us come back to life ecstatically. Sometimes we find ourselves to be alone but then we discover, surprisingly, that we are immensely strong, ready to take on life as it comes.

I have also dabbled in the ethos of nature and found that it has nothing but to offer us love. The river, the forests, the sun, the sea, the land, the clouds, the waterfalls, the mountains, all are continuously showering love and sending beautiful life lessons to us. We simply need to listen to them and they can make life so much easier to live.

I have also tried to pen down what my quirky mind captures in everyday life. My everyday car rides to office, my weekend naps laced with the anxiety of the coming week's busyness, my views of the city, lit with lamps, while I travel back from office. My odd visits to city's art museums and an attempt to define art, my concerns for the lives spent in the city's backstreets, my identification of lonely women in the society and their plight, even if it is a beautiful lady in red gown in an upmarket restaurant. Time spent in Mumbai's most famous restaurants shows so much about the society, when you observe in relaxation - people making merry, the allure and the sadness in their dimly lit lanterns and desperate attempt to drown loneliness in the city's liquor holes.

Oh... but I have also tried to counter my own cynicism by capturing the festive spirit punctuating the sadness of life and my personal pleasures in spending brilliant brainstorming sessions in the very attractive cafeterias of the city in an attempt to live life by the moments.

Last but not the least, the hopeless romantic that I am, how can I avoid writing about romance. All the pain and pleasures, the pregnant silence, the voluble exuberance, the wait and the meet, and finally to get lost in a euphoria from where no one wants to return.

Contents

Bits and pieces of philosophy

An Ode to Talent

Fortuitously driven into dreams of demonic texture,
For extreme passion has never been considered to be the noblest stricture;

Forever controlling the elements of force,
Sometimes blow out of proportions the dull life ordained;

Difficulty encountered by the ordinary to settle,
With the enormous strokes on time it prevails;

Ordinary folks with ordinary lives,
Seeking life to end in ordinary grey,

Dazzled by extremes of light and darkness,
Gets blinded anyway;

Reacting illogically to life and living,
And to experiencing life all along the way!

Let's Talk about Humanity

The unsafe tragedy of queer realizations,
That swarm on you as you plough through life,
Bothers you mysteriously as you inch through non-malleable iron minds;

Time made precious for reflections,
For reflections are to be least valued,
Blunt brashness is the call of the day,
Where humanity is knocked off for the day!

Life Prepares a Drink

Montages and mausoleums,
All a record of life;

Fascinating styles, art and pleasure,
For the spectators of life;

Witnessing the beautiful treasures of life;
Breathing the heavy aroma of life;

We are all intoxicated with the measures life pours;
Eternally drunk with the enchantment of life!

The Sphinx

The twist, the turn, the ecstasy burn!
Find your way in true return!

Voice of volcano makes a roar,
You never intend to be on the floor!

But still the gallons pour,
Your very being is in a throw!

Inside the world the fire burns,
The singe, the scar, the black peel darn!

Roasted almonds on a desert drip;
The scorch, the heat, the absolute retreat!

Rebellion

I am not feeling like writing anymore,
Envelop myself in Somerset Maugham!

With bitter dreams my surroundings preen,
Life's estimates need a screen!

World's views clash with my own reviews,
Clashes and fights are what my lot brews!

My opinions grow stronger,
When society acts a wringer!

As a cactus on an arid land,
Makes the impossible to stand!

Mind Control

You have a tendency to control your mind.
But how much can you actually control?

It decides to have its own flings,
And its own series of breakdowns,

It seems that the mind has a mind of its own,
Which you and me have nothing to say much upon;

Audaciousness and desperateness,
Crookedness and frustratedness!

You have to bear its whims and fancies,
All its drama and deliriousness!

The prank that it plays on your heart,
It comes to the brink of a new start!

It fools and cloys with your pain,
As though you have ignorance ingrained!

Mercilessly it treats you as foolish,
As if, it is its right to be churlish!

The entire monkey business is its,
Till death puts an end to it!

So can we conclude that we had a nice time with our mind,
During our entire miserable lifetime?

A Fresh Mind

Today morning I had a fresh mind,
But how fresh a mind can you keep?
Bereft of unpolluted rain,
In dearth of the fresh wild green!

But how fresh a mind can you keep?
In these concrete lands and artificial brands,
Superfluous and superficial all!

How fresh a mind can you keep?
When man is scared in the fear of all,
When he fails to pull up a defence against surrendering to all!

How fresh a mind can you keep?
When asked to hide your mind from your face,
Create destruction in thyself to please!

How fresh a mind can you keep?
When you are told that if you don't please, you don't belong to us all,
If you don't step into the traps that we have laid for you, you don't belong to us all!

So how do you keep your mind fresh?
Has been a question eternally asked.
And the answer had always been to master courage for not belonging to all!

The Calling

The distant land beckons,
On the shores of the stretching sea;
The port harkens the exit,
For a journey to be free;
No one accompanies me on the journey,
For the journey needs to be taken alone;
Nevertheless, the heart is warm with the feeling,
That at the end will someone be,
To receive and comfort me and make me sleep to my end!

Reincarnation

Life in the making,
Life in the breaking,
Life starts to end,
But is there a start to the end again?

Another chance, another opportunity,
To live the way, we love?

So the search for the eternity begins,
So the search for the eternal is there.

Everything vanishes,
Everything disappears,
To be hopefully found in the end;

But the eternal is always illusory,
No man has ever got its reality,
So the pain throbs in the heart,
Eternally in search for the start.

The Fume

Immeasurable, unaccountable, unacceptable heights!
Blowing off fuse in the night time;
Stale stomach in a rhapsody;
Montages of past lives and future,
Creating images of resurrection!
Psychedelic faces on the flow,
Trans music immeasurably slow!
Putrid perfume portendly pour,
Grasshopper dies on a green growth;
It is a substance world that maze creates,
Everything falling slow,
Neon lights on the glow;
Take me to the shore,
Where out of bound the distance seems,
I will awake some day and find for sure,
What is my existential cure?

Redemption

The pain, the pleasure, the ardent feel,
A mix of all is the life's deal;
Compromise or choose is the life's challenge,
Destiny smiles at the rear end;

To step out bold and face the blast,
Or blast your inner self, to be converted into dust;
Lustfulness to be blasted,
Or blast with lustfulness;

Which way life would measure your fill?
Full of dust or full of blast?
Both ways lead to redemption?
Or redemption to be redeemed with trust?

A Game called Life

The morning promises another day;
Who is going to take over today?

Who is going to win today?
How all it happens in the run of the day?

Who loses all and who gains all?
Is it some kind of game at play?

Play the game, play the game!
Till you lose it all again!

Chances are taken, chances will be taken;
Because we wish to win it all!

In life and in death,
We desire to remain ahead of all!

Freedom

I always felt I am in a prison gateway;
My heart is always looking for a break away;

Why that eternal desire to break free?
Haunts the mind, is a mystery!

Why do I feel the bondage so strong?
Why do I feel the shackles so hard?

What is this eternal craving and restlessness?
To get freedom from this worldliness?

Why there is no home for this heart?
Destined to be a universe farer from the start?

To become the dust and feel nothing,
And enjoy the eternal float is everything!

The Human Fear

One who is sleeping in a sleepless night,
Sleep is forbidden for some in the night;

Secretively drowned in thoughts forever,
Waking up in between to relive a drowning terror;

There the existential crisis holds the human mind;
Makes unsure the vision of future always on the grind;

The fear pulverizes human confidence premature,
Of anything that is of matter to his surviving nature.

An Ode to the Warrior

I have not killed my heart,
For I stoke the fire alive;
It is a journey worth remembering,
When you have crossed the shadowed terrain;
Snow, storm and rain,
All part of the journey;
The more you travel life,
The more the warrior you be!

Memoirs

What is the use of living?
After you have already lived.

In poems and verses you can continue,
But much less matters after you have left the venue.

Why aspire to live in people's minds,
When you don't live to see yourself in their minds?

People die, memories die,
Everything headed for dying,

For living the day is all that matters,
And this the truth no one shatters.

The Philosophical Laugh

The dark recesses of mind,
Whenever it goes on bright angelic rides,
Inner power of pain and radiance,
Exist side by side.
Polemical reads of philosophical guides,
Drive us into delirious pride,
Ennobled human kind has searched the soul,
And lost and found the eternity so foul,
That kept intangible peace at bay,
And rest of the other things in the grey.

Nature

Oh Riverine Riverine

The rivers that criss-crosses the delta prime,
Flowing on the earth, supine and serpentine,

Rushes of mud water and life,
In puddles and splashes, the lands lay rife,

Pushing its way through ample graze,
Soil and fertility oozing maze,

Forests and plants laughing loud,
With the windy breeze dancing proud,

Fortune's love plenty lay,
As nature's grace, without a pray.

The Setting Sun

The sun is about to set,
But will it take some more time to set?
Is it moving too fast to set?
As if on a rollercoaster ride to set.

Or is it taking a long time to set?
Bit by bit, minute by minute,
Fearing the moment of setting,
Of disappearing from the face of the earth,
And never to come back again?

The Dirty Beach

The cold shaft of wind,
From the sea running wild,
Beaches dirty and cold,
All open and there in the afternoon light.

How would it hide its shame?
Or has it become so shameless,
Announcing its dirt in front of all?
Knowing well, its innocence is always debated by all!

Miserable and pathetic is its condition;
The beach lies stark and naked!
And asks the entire world,
Who shall pay for it all?

Land and the Sea

Come and love me;
Embrace me and cuddle me;
Says the land to the sea.

With thousand waves,
I would like to embrace you,
Kiss you and love you;
Says the sea to the land.

The land says,
Your passion is deep;
Your passion is voluminous;
Your passion is a roller coaster ride;
It sinks me, it floats me;
It engulfs me and soaks me;

I lose my shape;
I lose my form;
I lose my entire being;
Oh sea, that I came so close to you;
Nurture me when you can!

Light and Darkness

Cloud, cloud, cloud!
The onerous cloud,
The remover of sunshine;
The usherer of dark;

You believe you bring peace and relief from the stark sun?
Just to tell there is comfort in the dark;
And pain under the sun?

Makes us think;
Where are we most comfortable?
In the light or the dark?

Can we get lost in the absolute light?
Can we get lost in absolute dark?
Or do we need both a little to keep us alive?

The Wild Wild Sea

The furious shattering rain,
In the bleak sea of mooning sunshine;

The rough sea at its edges,
Holding on to enormous grudges;

Lashing the shores in delight,
The human angst and its plight;

The sonorous music delights,
Roars of laughter for growing wild;

Nature's spirit on the rile,
Inspiring human souls of rank and file;

To brave the tempest,
Smother the sheep within,
And roar in the fest of life.

The Rushing Rapid On the Go

Waterfall gushing down,
Rushing down the hills,
Crossing the forests,
Sparkling flowing rushes;
Making wet the hill side,
They pour down with enormous flow;
Nature's exuberance on the flow,
Resounding sound in the cloud;
Each current in competition with the other,
For an unknown destination that no one bothers,
Flowing with such unbridled energy,
To pounce and pound on the earth around;
Breaking everything in pieces,
Shattering them to ground earth and nothingness,
Reflection of the flow of life on the go,
Mercilessly pulverizing man's own ego!

The Rain Forest

The green forests beckon,
To its mysterious dark foliage;
The rain drenched trees;
The water washed hillside,
All wet and fresh;
Wets my mind and spirit,
To a solution ready for soluble love,
To remain all soggy in emotion,
Gives me back my life!

The Horizon

Lush green layout,
On the low mountain stretch;
Dark looming clouds,
Creating soft sombre light,
Falling on the dark deep folds,
Of the light green mountain side;

The horizon and the mountain outline,
Kiss each other in the sky,
As lovers in deep embrace,
Inseparable from their entwining frames,
Witnessing light and darkness with equal grace!

Beloved for ever, the mountain reaches for the sky,
Eager to mesh with the horizon and blend in the sky;
Forever the horizon remains attached with the mountain,
For it feels its duty to be there,
Sun and cloud are irrelevant,
For the horizon to be there!

Exhilaration

The sea still and deep;
The music smooth and rhythmic;

Souls beautiful, soulful and thoughtful;
Waves in every sinew of body and is mindful;

Small waves with tremor and power;
To burst open on the surface with a shower!

Nature's rhythms at play everywhere;
Unknown, unobserved but continuously there;

The beauty, shimmer and sunshine on the sea;
The palms, on the waves of air, dances with glee;

The pulsation of life and its curious rhythms;
The thrill to get lost in it all with furious freedom;

The Bird that took its Flight

The endless journey begins,
In the white and light of the air;

In the vast oceans of nowhere,
Find me if you can in the vastness of the fare;

I stare long and hard at the distance;
All calm and cool through the lens;

Where the blue merges with the blue,
And no other particular hue;

Why settle for any less?
When flying is all that I have to do.

The Rising Sun

The golden shimmer on the waters lay,
The morning sunlight is brightest in May.

The golden sea reflects the rising sun,
As the king on the throne of a thousand tonne;

So much gold it adds to the golden heart,
Those who can appreciate the colour of nature's art.

Magically feeling the warmth and the shine,
For the thousand past lives at the feet of this shrine.

Everyday life

The Dreamy Drowsy Car Rides

Every morning it happens in a routine way,
Gliding past shops and slums on the way,
Gliding past some barren lands in the midway.

Over the flyover driving smooth as if on a ramble,
A little like a child's enchantment in a cradle,
Still awakens that thrill and a skipping babble.

Destination immaterial to the journey as always,
Because the destination remains constant any ways,
It is the ride which is enjoyable and the rest is forgettable!

Lady in Red Gown

Fair and straight and stunning,
Beauty all over is burning!
Wealth and status at every step,
She belongs to the class of crest!

But the shadow behind the veneer,
Is it some kind of sneer?
Anxiousness archetypal,
Fear in the marble citadel?

Why search for validation,
When nature has bequeathed admiration?
The nervous act of haughty,
Is a frivolous act of sorority.

One Summer Afternoon in Leopold Café

The warm air around,
Sweat trickling down,
The enormous hall,
Pictures on the wall.

60s and 70s, archaic hey!
Lots of Marilyn Monroe on the fray,
Asking for attention when she made hay!

One gets lost in the past,
To be brought back to the present,
With the zest of the crowd in this admirable nest!

People strange and from distant lands,
Mingling equally with the natives of the land;
Clatter and clanker of dishes china and cutlery steel,
Rolls of laughter and loud voices on the reel;
Makes the heat escalate further,
My wait amidst such weather,
In this warm heat and summer fervour,
In formals and decent dress, is an experience forever.

My Lethargic Bliss

It is evening time,
And I draw the curtains to the day's activities;
Autumn wind and clear sky,
October round the corner,
The pretty chirpings of the birds around,
And the sounds of gaiety of a Sunday evening,
My feelings of lethargy and bliss,
Of a late afternoon nap,
Makes me take a dull look at life,
With a faint fear of busy week to come,
To take my lethargic bliss away!

City Lights

The city lit in light,
Masquerading all in shine.

Pretty lights, large lights,
All across the town they shine.

Shadow around each light,
Interesting bits they hide.

The desperation and the fight,
The perspiration and the snide.

The heartlessness of the failed,
The ruthlessness of the trade.

The light clings onto the shadow,
For it finds comfort in its meadow.

And doesn't dare to live alone,
And is shy to be on its own!

An Attempt to Define Art

Table's décor and fine arts display,
The portrayals and betrayals of humans in dismay,
The frayed music of the accordion's tunes,
The pain in hearts of disastrous ruins.

Artistry for art's sake,
Stakes are high for the fake,
The smile, the stance, the gaiety,
The pretentiousness so mighty.

The drama in every drama,
One peeks through the other,
One sees the other and rues,
Am I missing out on the other?

City Nights

The night ushers in a dark retreat,
Midnight blues in the backs of streets;
Tortured souls in a drowsy stupor,
Hold on to breath in the mist of vapour;

Vanishing light at the end of the road,
Around dimly lit lamps the darkness so broad;
Every material being on the pry,
Hope or disappointment raise a cry;

Love shall you be squished forever,
From the souls a hue darker;
Denizens on whom darkness prey,
Where allowance of light is a pray;

A Partying Society

The crowd, the crowd, the flirty crowd;
The sensation and the hype;
The pretty faces, the skin fair;
Amor in the eyes;

The mesmerizing effect;
The convincing, the denial;
The coquetry and the endorsement;
The mute exchanges of the bleary-eyed and the absent minded;

All lost in their own thoughts;
In the thoughts lost forever;
Light headed intoxication;
Everyone busy with their fixation;

Who looks at whom?
And who thinks of whom?
All muddled and confused and murky in the rhythm;
All lose trail in the air!

The Lonely Woman

The lonely woman on the horizon;
Breeze on her face,
Light in her eyes.
The travel through rough terrain;
Is what is all her plight;
When and when will she take a turn?
The world keeps wondering,
Will she settle for the horizon or look up at the sky?

Restobar

The crackling light on sparkling glasses;
Wine, dine and cutlery fine;
The potency of powerlessness in every drop of vintage;
On display on the racks of heritage;
Invitation galore to spikes of happiness;
Life is but a sweet sour culinary delight, with drops of delightful forgetfulness!

Evening Mood

Sadness in the lantern deep,
My voice in the sadness grieve;

Pain and grace jostle close,
Allowing me to wallow low;

Late evening light mellows slow,
Melting in the light of the lanterns' glow;

I wander at the boats moving slow,
On the stream of sunshine in the evening glow;

My life stands still,
In the flow of the timing slow;

The Recess

In a dark corner of a dungeon closed,
Where spirits hung in the air,

No, it is not a haunted house,
Although the picture similar to the phrase!

The pigeon hole for liquor and survival,
For modern human's weekend revival;

The succour for endless stiff corporate life,
A dungeon doused in gallons provide the life;

The cosy comfort of mingling crowd,
To mix and merge in the bumbling shroud,

Is a source of life and danger too;
The fine fabric of modern society brews!

The Drums that Beat and the Hearts that Soar

The drums beat in rhythms,
Gods bid farewell to demons;

The light-hearted spirit dances in madness,
The intoxicated air tremble with dusty daringness;

The whirl in the wind,
The swirl in the mind,

The fervour created,
For the lust to be coveted;

All for a luscious taste of life,
Incredible attempt at feeling alive!

The Cafeteria

This is a cafeteria,
Where I would like to sit and drink and smoke,
And think of the world through the tinted glass door!

Mega thoughts would churn up mega ideas!
Interrupted with lover's kisses on the brow!

I would sit still and gather ideas,
Which only these kinds of places throw!
Manifesting the life moribund in my smoky vision slow.

The soft food and soft glow,
And the soft of the liquor slow,
Ideally the artist's place,
To shape and churn and grow!

The City from a Distance

The still blue water,
Under the broken bridge;

Ancient structure and architecture
Through the threads of birch's shades;

Tall spires of cathedral reaching high,
The city feels intact in red and yellow dye;

A dance and a song by the riverside dale,
Quite a picturesque frame of an ancient tale;

The city so perfect and pale from distance deem,
But who knows its whereabouts in the interior scene?

Romance

Falling in Love

When I fall in love with someone, I fall very, very deep;

Down dark crevices,
And cold iced showers,
The fear of the fierceness,
Of the pitch black dark;

When I fall in love with someone, I fall very, very deep;

The stifled cries,
The aching heart,
The stunted thoughts,
The shooting pain fraught;

When I fall in love with someone, I fall very, very deep;

But I fall over and over again,
And a countless number of times do I fall,
For there is nothing more intoxicating,
Than a deep, deep fall;

When I fall in love with someone, I fall very, very deep

It tears apart my heart,
It tears apart my soul,
But I still want to fall,
For it keeps me in thrall;

When I fall in love with someone, I fall very, very deep;

The Seaside Silence

The still sea;
The green bobbing boat;
The roof top beer;
White yacht dots on still blue water,
Quite a sight for the lazy green eyes.
Warmth and the pain,
All engulfing vain;
The wrought iron curves,
The curves of the skin,
The small curves of the water,
The curved strain of romance,
So much could have been said;
Yet the untold remained unsaid....

Instinct

Looks so handsome and incredulous,
Tingling nerves of love and vapour.
Rising in the body of a mesmerized creature,
There is so much in the darkness of those eyes,
One gets lost in the chaos of its chaotic vibes;
The stillness in the looks are magnetic and dark attraction,
Getting lost in the folds of its shadowy traction,
Deep and far away the siren's refrain,
From where you return or do not return,
The mysterious calling of life and its deep darkness,
The exhilaration of getting lost in total blackness.

Meeting of Souls

Lost in thought
Oh you! miserable thoughts!
Fuelled with passion and caresses;
Drenched in sadness and expectations;
The mortal sits still bound up all by love,
Never knowing when the call would come;
Waiting eternally in the moment for the beckoning;
Always imagining the togetherness and the comfort;
Lives strung together in the eternity of time,
Together realizing the existence of soul.
Here and now and anywhere in time,
The meeting of the inseparable souls,
Speech frozen, blood frozen the indolence strong and acute,
Life's sweet existence in the intoxicating trance…

Love Sick

Lost in love;
Lust in love;
Sick and feverish in love;
Undressed and dressed in love;
So full of passion in love,
Oh so full of love,
So much so happy in the union,
That don't know,
What is mine anymore;
What is me anymore;
That is so much of liberation;
That is so much of peace;
That stop thinking of anything,
And surrender to the stillness of nothing.

Music by the Sea

The music that goes on playing,
Till the sunset and the dawn;
More whispers in the ears of my beloved,
It's magical and forlorn;
My passion beats the metres,
My crooning touches the chord;
I sway my head in happiness,
To be one with the one!

www.ingramcontent.com/pod-product-compliance
Ingram Content Group UK Ltd.
Pitfield, Milton Keynes, MK11 3LW, UK
UKHW021400190726
13845UKWH00028B/793

9 789390 034789